Earth's Changing Climate

Living with Climate Change

WORLD
BOOK

World Book
a Scott Fetzer company
Chicago

For information about other World Book publications, visit our website at www.worldbook.com or call 1-800-WORLDBK (967-5325).

For information about sales to schools and libraries, call 1-800-975-3250 (United States) or 1-800-837-5365 (Canada).

World Book, Inc.
233 N. Michigan Ave. Suite 2000
Chicago, IL 60601
U.S.A.

Library of Congress Cataloging-in-Publication Data

Living with climate change.
    pages cm. -- (Earth's changing climate)
  Includes index.
  Summary: "Explores ways that people can reduce their use of fossil fuels, and thereby reduce the amount of greenhouse gases emitted, and ways to adapt to a warming world; includes glossary, additional resources, and index."-- Provided by publisher.
    ISBN 978-0-7166-2713-5
    1. Climatic changes--Economic aspects--Juvenile literature. 2. Climatic changes--Social aspects--Juvenile literature. 3. Economic development--Environmental aspects--Juvenile literature. 4. Sustainable development--Juvenile literature. I. World Book, Inc.
    QC903.15.L58 2016
    363.7--dc23
                          2015028051

Living with Climate Change ISBN: 978-0-7166-2713-5
Earth's Changing Climate Set ISBN: 978-0-7166-2705-0
E-book ISBN: 978-0-7166-2723-4 (ePUB3 format)

Printed in China by Toppan Leefung Printing Ltd., Guangdong Province
1st printing October 2015

Staff

Writer: Will Adams

Executive Committee
President
Jim O'Rourke

Vice President and Editor in Chief
Paul A. Kobasa

Vice President, Finance
Donald D. Keller

Director, International Sales
Kristin Norell

Director, Human Resources
Bev Ecker

Editorial

Manager, Annuals/Series Nonfiction
Christine Sullivan

Editor, Annuals/Series Nonfiction
Kendra Muntz

Manager, Science
Jeff De La Rosa

Editors, Science
Will Adams
Echo Gonzalez

Administrative Assistant Annuals/Series Nonfiction
Ethel Matthews

Manager, Contracts & Compliance (Rights & Permissions)
Loranne K. Shields

Manager, Indexing Services
David Pofelski

Manufacturing/ Production

Manufacturing Manager
Sandra Johnson

Production/Technology Manager
Anne Fritzinger

Proofreader
Nathalie Strassheim

Graphics and Design

Senior Art Director
Tom Evans

Senior Designers
Matt Carrington
Isaiah Sheppard
Don Di Sante

Manager, Cartographic Services
Wayne K. Pichler

Senior Cartographer
John M. Rejba

Acknowledgments

Alamy Images: 13 (H. Mark Weidman Photography), 31 (Bernhard Classen), 37 (Ed Darack), 45 (Stephen Foster). AP Photo: 25 (PRNewsFoto/SolarReserve), 33 (Michael Bell, The Canadian Press). Getty Images: 35 (Eric Bouvet, Gamma-Rapho). iStockphoto: 11 (bjones27), 17 (Anna Bryukhanova), 27 (Ron Thomas). Matarozzi/Pelsinger Builders, Inc.: 15 (Matthew Millman). Science Source: 29 (Maximilian Stock), 39 (Victor Habbick Visions). Shutterstock: 5 (Tatiana Grozetskaya), 7 (BKMCphotography), 9 (PromesaArtStudio), 19 (TFoxFoto), 21 (Yusef El-Mansouri), 23 (atm2003), 43 (Wollertz). U.S. Department of Agriculture: 41 (Stephen Ausmus).

Table of contents

A wind turbine generates electricity without emissions that cause climate change.

© Anawat Sudchanham, Shutterstock

Glossary There is a glossary of terms on page 46. Terms defined in the glossary are in type **that looks like this** on their first appearance on any spread (two facing pages).

Introduction

Climate change is a serious threat to all living things on Earth. Today, scientists think that changes in climate have begun to take place because of the *greenhouse effect*. The greenhouse effect is caused by **carbon dioxide** (CO_2) and other gases in Earth's **atmosphere.** Just as the blanket on your bed traps some of your body heat, these gases trap heat near Earth. Huge amounts of carbon dioxide released when people burn **fossil fuels** contribute to this greenhouse effect. The changes are causing a rise in global average temperatures called *global warming*.

The extra heat could ruin **habitats** or cause damaging weather events. The problem will only get worse in the future. Even if we stopped releasing large amounts of CO_2 into the air today, the world would continue to warm for many years to come.

How can humans lessen and live with the effects of climate change? One way is for people to think about reducing what is called their **carbon footprint.** This is the amount of CO_2 a person makes through his or her actions. By shrinking our carbon footprints, we can reduce the amount of CO_2 escaping into the atmosphere, combating the greenhouse effect. Humans may also combat climate change in other ways, such as making changes to Earth or its atmosphere, but these methods are more difficult.

4

Factory smokestacks emit carbon dioxide and other **greenhouse gases** into the air.

Fighting climate change at home

Greenhouse gases released into the air, called *emissions* (ih MIHSH uhnz), are a big problem. They are a major cause of climate change. But people can help reduce these emissions by making small changes around the house. Many of these changes cost little or nothing and can even save money in the long run.

For example, most of the energy used in a house goes to heating and cooling. Often, that energy comes from burning **fossil fuels** at power plants. These fuels produce **carbon dioxide** (CO_2), which causes global warming. By turning the furnace down to a cooler temperature during winter or the air conditioner up to a slightly warmer temperature in summer, people can reduce the amount of energy used.

A difference of a few degrees in each house can help reduce carbon emissions a lot.

Global warming vs. climate change

The words *global warming* and *climate change* are often used to mean the same thing. These words are used to mean two very closely linked ideas. Global warming is the recent, *observed* (noticed) increase in **average global surface temperatures** on Earth. Climate change means the changes in **climate** linked to changes in average global temperature. Global average temperature has a complicated effect on climate. Global warming will not cause every place to get warmer. Instead, it will have a variety of effects on temperature, rain and snow, and other parts of climate. These effects are together called *climate change.*

A home furnace works by burning fossil fuels, giving off greenhouse gases in the process.

Energy-efficient light bulbs

A thing that is *efficient* is able to work well without wasting energy. Light bulbs that are energy efficient are another good way to reduce energy use in the home. Many people still use incandescent (IHN kuhn DEHS uhnt) bulbs to light their homes. This kind of bulb was invented over 100 years ago. Incandescent bulbs make light by heating a wire inside the bulb until the wire glows. Much of the energy these bulbs use is wasted as heat. Also, an average incandescent light bulb lasts for only about 1,000 hours of use before it burns out.

Newer kinds of bulbs use less electricity and can last far longer. Fluorescent lights, for instance, use electricity to *excite* (energize) a gas in a glass tube. The excited gas causes the tube to glow. This process uses less electricity than heating a wire. Compact fluorescent light (CFL) bulbs need only 15 **watts** of energy to produce the same light as a 60-watt incandescent bulb.

Light-emitting diode (LED) bulbs use solid materials that give off light when electricity runs through them. An LED bulb uses just 12 watts to produce the same amount of light as a 60-watt incandescent bulb. These bulbs can last for up to 25,000 hours of use.

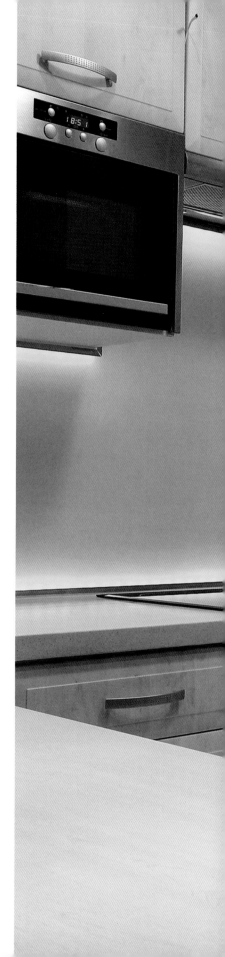

Other uses for LED's

LED lights are useful in many ways, not just for home lighting. They are used in energy-saving flat-screen TV's, street lights, traffic signals, vehicle headlights, and even as runway lights at airports.

How can one person make a difference?

Greenhouse gas *emissions* (gases released to Earth's **atmosphere**) are a big problem. How can changes made by one person make a difference? It's true that one person's actions have very little effect on Earth's atmosphere. But, many people making small changes can add up to produce big, helpful results.

For instance, imagine if each household in the United States replaced an incandescent light bulb with a new, energy-efficient bulb. This could reduce emissions by the same amount as taking half a million cars off the road! And that's only changing out one light bulb per home. Imagine how large the reduction in greenhouse gas emissions would be if people replaced all of their old-fashioned bulbs with LED bulbs.

People can also make better decisions when they shop. For example, some companies make a special effort to use business practices that are friendly to the **environment.** In buying from such companies, people can choose goods that are better for the Earth.

Such small actions as carrying groceries in reusable bags can make a difference to the environment. A single reusable bag may take less energy to manufacture than hundreds of disposable bags.

Building to use less energy

There are many other ways to reduce the production of **greenhouses gases** that are causing global warming and **climate** change. Architects are people who *design* buildings. That means they plan what the buildings will look like and how they will be built. Architects come up with new ways to reduce the **carbon footprint** of buildings all of the time.

Most of these methods involve designing or changing buildings in certain ways so that they take less energy to heat and cool. For example, buildings can be built so that they make better use of the sun for light and heat. One way to do this is by having many windows face in the direction that receives the most sunlight for that region. Then, during winter days, the sun streams through the windows and warms building materials that were specially chosen to hold heat. Such materials include **concrete** used for flooring. These materials are said to have a high *thermal mass*. This means a building material is good for storing, then releasing heat. The flooring continues to release heat at night.

Windows shown here were designed and placed to catch the most sunlight to help light and heat the building.

Energy-smart buildings

A lot of energy can be saved by designing houses and other buildings to be more energy efficient. Many energy-saving ideas were used in 2010 to construct the Matarozzi/Pelsinger Multi-Use Building in San Francisco, California.

The building was an old warehouse that was turned into an office building. Just the decision to reuse an old building, rather than tearing it down and building a new one, in itself prevented emissions. The heavy machinery required to tear down the warehouse and make new construction materials would have released a lot of **greenhouse gases.**

In changing the building, the architects reused many of the original building parts, saving both money and **carbon dioxide** (CO_2) emissions. They also covered the windows with metal sheets with small holes in them. These sheets provide privacy and protect against the sun's glare and heat. They lower cooling costs while still allowing in light and air. Part of the parking lot of the old building was removed to create an outdoor garden. Bicycle parking was built to encourage employees to bike to work instead of driving.

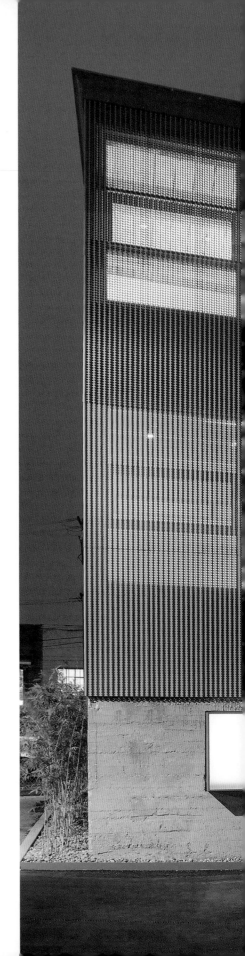

The Matarozzi/Pelsinger Multi-Use Building in San Francisco is an energy-smart building.

Reusing and recycling materials

Creating new building materials always releases some amount of greenhouse gases. Construction materials take energy to make and to transport. Making new concrete, for example, takes a huge amount of energy. Reusing or recycling materials is often more energy efficient than using new materials in a building.

Efficient cars and trucks

Moving people and things around is a major source of **carbon dioxide** (CO_2) emissions. Most cars and trucks use motors that burn gasoline. We will always need transportation—ways to move people and things around—but we can find ways to lower the **carbon footprint** of transportation by using energy-efficient cars and trucks.

For example, some cars and trucks use electric motors as well as gasoline engines. These are called *hybrid electric vehicles,* and they produce fewer CO_2 emissions. The driver still has to fill up at the gas pump, but the vehicle's electric battery kicks in to help the motor when speeding up. This means that the engine burns less gasoline. When less power is needed for driving, the motor recharges the battery.

Some cars now have no gasoline engine at all. Instead, they rely completely on battery-powered electric motors. Batteries are very good at storing energy. Only about 25 percent an electric car's energy goes to waste. Gasoline-powered cars waste about 75 percent of the energy in the fuel. Electric cars release less CO_2 into the **atmosphere.**

But electric cars do need electric power to charge, which can result in CO_2 emissions from power plants. If the car is charged in an area where electric power is made using fossil fuels, it can actually have a larger carbon footprint than a hybrid electric vehicle. So people must choose carefully when they decide what kind of car to drive.

Mass transit

Taking **mass transit** instead of driving is another great way to reduce your **carbon footprint.** Many people drive alone in their cars to work or shop. But many cities have mass transit systems that include buses, streetcars, and trains. With mass transit, many people ride together. It can be cheaper to take mass transit than it is to drive.

Although the motor on a large bus or a train produces more **carbon dioxide** (CO_2) emissions than that of a single car, the emissions released per passenger are lower. An average bus or train passenger saves over 4,000 pounds (2,000 kilograms) of CO_2 emissions a year compared to driving alone in a car.

Many cities are now purchasing new buses and trains that are more energy efficient. Some newer buses run on natural gas. While natural gas is a **fossil fuel,** it produces less CO_2 when burned than do other fuels, like gasoline. Other buses have hybrid motors that use gasoline and batteries.

Mass transit creates other benefits, too. It reduces the number of cars on the road, which in turn improves traffic. And, fewer cars stuck in traffic means less CO_2 in the air. People who use mass transit are also more likely to walk or bike to or from the station or bus stop. They get some healthy exercise as well!

Even better than mass transit

Although taking mass transit is more efficient than driving, walking or biking is more efficient still. Walking or biking for short trips is a great way to reduce your carbon footprint—and to get some exercise, too!

Mass transit buses in Portland, Oregon, in the northwestern United States

Change in Los Angeles

Los Angeles, California, is a huge U.S. city on the Pacific Coast. It is often thought of as a car-centered city. Freeways crisscross the city and surrounding **suburbs.** The sprawling city's **mass transit** system has had a troubled past.

Many private companies sprang up to offer mass transit service as the city grew. Suburbs were built along streetcar lines that connected them to the heart of the city. But most of these transit companies went out of business as Los Angeles grew and its citizens began to prefer cars. As Los Angeles streets and highways became increasingly crowded, however, city planners realized that the city needed to spend money on mass transit.

In 1993, after decades of failed plans, Los Angeles finally opened its first **subway.** The city is currently planning more subway and bus routes. Because Los Angeles is so spread out compared to other large cities, it may never reach a large number of mass transit riders. But the mass transit added to the city has given people a way to avoid driving. It has also reduced traffic jams on city streets and lowered **carbon dioxide** (CO_2) emissions.

20

People board the subway in Los Angeles.

Solar power

The sun sends an enormous amount of energy to Earth. This energy can be converted into electric power that we can use, called *solar power.* Solar power produces no **greenhouse gases** at all. It can help reduce the use of power plants that generate electric power by burning such **fossil fuels** as coal.

The most common way to make solar power is with *solar cells.* Solar cells are made of a special material that gives off electric current when light shines on it. Solar cells produce only a small amount of energy compared to other sources. But they are small and have no moving parts, so they can be put almost anywhere there is sunlight to make electric power with little maintenance.

Power plants that make large amounts of electric power from solar energy can also be built. They work best in sunny areas with few cloudy days.

Solar cells on the roof of this house generate electric power.

Energy from the sun

People burn fossil fuels to produce around 12 trillion **watts** of electricity worldwide. That is a lot of energy, but it is nothing compared to the amount of energy the sun produces. Of the energy the sun gives off, more than 150 quadrillion watts reaches Earth each day. (A quadrillion is a one followed by 15 zeroes.) That's thousands of times more energy than humans use.

Crescent Dunes

Nevada, a state in the southwest United States, recently built the Crescent Dunes Solar Power Plant. The plant is expected to make enough electric power for 75,000 houses without producing any **greenhouse gases** at all. The power plant is scheduled to begin making electric power by the end of 2015.

This new solar power plant uses moving mirrors called **heliostats.** These mirrors are controlled so that they face the sun and direct its rays toward a tall tower. In most solar power plants, sunlight is used to heat a huge container of water to boiling. The boiling water makes steam that is used to spin large **turbines** that make electric power.

However, Crescent Dunes uses a different method. Its solar energy will instead heat *molten* (melted) salts. Heat from the molten salts is then used to boil water to generate electricity. Why add this extra step? The molten salts hold onto heat better than water does. This means that when the energy is not needed, the hot liquid can be stored in **insulated** tanks for later use. In this way, the new solar power plant will be able to produce electric power even at night or on cloudy days.

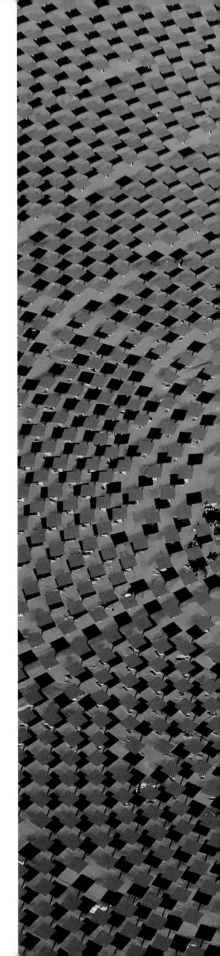

The tower with surrounding mirrors at the Crescent Dunes Solar Power Plant

Power storage

If other energy sources, such as solar power, can be used, why do we still burn coal and gas? Some of the reason is that other power sources are unpredictable. They may not always produce power when it is needed. For example, many solar power plants cannot produce electric power on a cloudy day or at night. For solar power to become more widely used, scientists must develop ways for it to deliver electric power around the clock.

Wind power

The motion of the wind can also be used to provide clean energy without making any **greenhouse gases.** If people could use only 10 percent of Earth's total wind energy, it would be far more than the energy we need every year. In addition, wind is a *renewable* energy source that can never run out, unlike **fossil fuels.**

Wind power is captured through the use of wind **turbines.** These are much the same as a windmill. The wind causes the propeller-like blades of the turbine to turn. The blades are connected to a shaft that powers a generator, making electric power. Some places have more windy days than other places do and are more suitable than others for wind power. Wind turbines can also be built offshore, to take advantage of strong ocean breezes.

Wind turbines are mounted on tall towers to keep the spinning blades in the stronger and steadier winds above ground level. The tall towers and spinning blades, however, can injure or kill birds. Also, large wind turbines make noise that can make them difficult to live around.

Even with these drawbacks, wind power is a good way to reduce greenhouse gas emissions. In fact, wind power already produces 2.6 percent of the energy used worldwide.

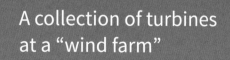

A collection of turbines at a "wind farm"

Which alternative energy is best?

There are many sources of energy other than **fossil fuels.** Together, these are called *alternative power* or *alternative energy.* (*Alternative* in these terms means *a different choice.*) Most alternative energy releases little or no **greenhouse gas.** Each has its own benefits and drawbacks.

Some alternative energy sources only work in certain areas. Wind farms are best placed in areas with strong, steady winds. *Geothermal* (JEE uh THUR muhl) is another type of energy—*geo* means *Earth* and *thermal* means *heat.* This kind of energy harnesses the heat from inside Earth. This heat can be changed into electric power in special plants. However, geothermal energy is only possible in certain areas, such as near volcanoes.

Hydroelectric power is electric power made using the motion of falling or flowing water. In a hydroelectric power plant, moving water spins a propeller-like device called a *water turbine.* The turbine's shaft drives an electric generator. Hydroelectric plants are best suited for areas with large rivers or strong tides.

A scientist works on a machine built to test the idea of nuclear fusion.

Nuclear fusion

If it can be achieved, *nuclear fusion* might be the "best" alternative power source. Nuclear fusion makes energy by combining **atoms.** This is the way the sun makes energy. But fusion is extremely complicated and requires a lot of energy to get started. Some people think that fusion power plants may never work. But if scientists can overcome the many difficulties, fusion would be a perfect energy source.

Capturing carbon

Carbon dioxide (CO_2) has been building up in Earth's **atmosphere** for decades. This buildup is contributing to global warming. Reducing emissions (the release of gases) helps, but our modern world runs on fossil fuels that produce those emissions. One solution is to capture CO_2 at the source, to prevent it from escaping into the atmosphere.

At power plants and other factories, special devices called *scrubbers* can separate CO_2 from other **exhaust** gases. The CO_2 is then stored to keep it out of the atmosphere. This process is called *carbon capture and storage* (CCS).

One CCS method is to *compress* (squeeze into a small space) the CO_2. The CO_2 is then *injected* (forced) into *porous* (spongy) rock deep beneath Earth's surface. The layers of rock prevent the CO_2 from leaking out. However, scientists do not know whether the gas might leak out one day.

Another method is called *mineral storage*. In **mineral** storage, CO_2 is combined with certain minerals found either underground or in industrial wastes. The CO_2 attaches to these minerals, so there is no risk of it leaking into the atmosphere. The reaction, however, takes a long time.

This coal power plant in Germany uses carbon capture and storage to produce clean energy.

Boundary Dam Power Station

In October 2014, a portion of the Boundary Dam Power Station in the Canadian province of Saskatchewan was rebuilt for carbon capture. The power plant burns coal, a **fossil fuel,** to generate electricity. Burning coal is a major source of **carbon dioxide** (CO_2).

Scrubbers were installed to remove most of the CO_2 from the plant **exhaust** so it is not released into the **atmosphere.** The process and equipment used for carbon capture at power plants can be expensive. But CO_2 has many uses in industry. So the power plant sells the CO_2 to a company that pumps it deep underground to help recover oil. The sale helps offset the cost of the carbon capture, while still making sure the CO_2 is stored away and not released.

Some people, however, question whether producing more oil with captured CO_2 is really helpful in solving the urgent problem of climate change. These people are concerned that such uses encourage people to use more oil by making it cheaper. Burning more oil causes yet more CO_2 to be released.

Carbon scrubbers at the
Boundary Dam Power Station

Is carbon capture and storage dangerous?

Not everyone thinks that carbon capture and storage (CCS) is a good idea. Some people worry that the stored **carbon dioxide** (CO_2) could escape because of leaks or earthquakes. Then, all the money and effort spent on CCS would be wasted.

Experts have found that pumping liquids and gases underground can itself cause small earthquakes. These quakes might damage communities around a CCS plant and cause CO_2 gas to leak out into the **atmosphere.** Large leaks could release huge amounts of carbon dioxide very quickly, leading to a disaster. Small amounts of carbon dioxide are harmless to breathe. But a large leak from a CCS facility could kill any people or animals nearby.

Some people also fear that CCS will give people a false sense of security. People might think that it is no longer important to reduce **greenhouse gas** production or improve energy efficiency if we can simply bury emissions in the ground. They believe it is better to focus on using less energy and producing less greenhouse gas.

Lake Nyos in 1986, after a large release of carbon dioxide killed many local people who lived around the lake

Lake Nyos disaster

Lake Nyos is a deep lake in Cameroon, West Africa. Volcanic activity naturally fills the lake with carbon dioxide. In August 1986, the lake released a huge volume of carbon dioxide, like a shaken soft drink. Over 1,700 people were killed in nearby villages. Scientists think that a major CCS leak could lead to a similar disaster.

Making changes to Earth

Geoengineering (JEE oh ᴇʜɴ juh NIHR eng) means making changes to Earth to *counteract* (turn back) the threats from **climate** change. Geoengineering projects would try to keep the temperature of Earth from rising in several ways. Two ways often discussed involve reducing the amount of energy Earth receives from the sun or directly removing **carbon dioxide** (CO_2) from the **atmosphere.**

Geoengineering projects would cost a lot of money because they would have to be large enough to affect the entire planet. Since they would affect everyone, they would also have to be approved by international agreement.

Such huge projects would likely cause some problems themselves. A project might change weather patterns and cause flooding or **drought** in some areas, for instance. But dealing with the effects of geoengineering projects could still be better than letting climate change take its course.

Humans already alter Earth in many ways, such as by shaping the land with machinery.

Blocking sunlight

One idea that geoengineers have had is to reflect some of the sun's energy back into space. For example, airplanes or balloons could spray special *aerosols* into the **atmosphere.** Aerosols are tiny *particles* (pieces) scattered in the air. The particles reflect sunlight back into space. That means there would be less heat from sunlight on Earth to be trapped by **greenhouse gases.** This would be one of the less costly geoengineering projects. But the aerosols eventually fall out of the atmosphere. They would have to be replaced over and over.

Another way to block sunlight would be to launch huge mirrors into orbit around Earth. These mirrors would reflect some of the sunlight headed toward Earth back out into space. Many people doubt this idea can work. Such mirrors would be very expensive to launch and maintain. Others have proposed that people can make Earth itself reflect more sunlight. This could be done by covering large areas with material that reflects sunlight.

These ideas may sound strange. But the **technology** to do such things is possible. Though possible, these ideas would, however, be difficult and expensive.

Volcanic cooling

Large volcanic eruptions can send ash and dust into the atmosphere and temporarily cool the planet. The idea of releasing aerosols into the atmosphere imitates this natural cooling action.

An artist imagines a space mirror over Earth.

Removing carbon dioxide

Some geoengineering solutions for **climate** change focus on removing **carbon dioxide** (CO_2) from the **atmosphere.** One way to remove it is to use machines that *absorb* (take in) CO_2 from the air. As with carbon capture and storage (CCS), the absorbed CO_2 would be injected underground.

People can also lock CO_2 away by making a material called *biochar*. Biochar is formed when **organic** materials are burned without **oxygen.** The carbon in the organic materials is then locked up in the material and cannot be released as CO_2 into the atmosphere. Huge airtight chambers can be set up to make large amounts of biochar. The biochar can easily be buried underground.

Another method proposed to remove CO_2 from the air is to **fertilize** Earth's oceans with iron. *Algae* (tiny plantlike organisms) that live in the open ocean need iron to grow and reproduce. Some scientists would like to try adding iron to ocean water to encourage certain types of algae to bloom, taking in CO_2 from the air in the process. When the algae die, some of them sink to the bottom of the ocean, taking the CO_2 they absorbed with them.

A scientist creates biochar in a laboratory.

Should we try geoengineering?

Geoengineering solutions to **climate** change problems would affect the entire Earth and every living being. For this reason, governments and people throughout the world would have to agree to their use. The exact effects of any single project are too complex and far-reaching to accurately predict. The effects may not always be positive, either.

For example, some areas might experience floods, **drought,** or other climate problems as a result of a particular geoengineering project. Many scientists fear the results from some projects could lead to disasters.

Many people are against geoengineering because it does not attack the root cause of climate change—the production of **greenhouse gases.** They warn that countries could bet on risky geoengineering programs that end up causing, rather than preventing, a disaster in the **environment.** They recommend investing in energy efficient **technology** and lessening greenhouse gas emissions instead.

Scientists are not sure how geoengineering will affect different places around the globe.

No quick fix

Many scientists and *environmentalists* (people who work to protect Earth and its **atmosphere**) are afraid that the public will see geoengineering as a "quick fix" to the problem of climate change. Really, there is no quick fix. Geoengineering may play some part in fighting climate change. But alternative energy and more efficient vehicles will also play a very large part.

International agreements to fight climate change

Because **climate** change involves the entire planet, all countries must work together to fight it. In 1997, some nations signed the Kyoto (kee OH toh) Protocol (PROH tuh kol), an international treaty to reduce **greenhouse gas** emissions. The countries that approved the treaty did reduce their emissions, but many other countries did not approve it. These countries included the two worst polluters—China and the United States. The Kyoto Protocol alone did little to stop global warming.

Some states, provinces, and countries have set their own goals. For example, the Pacific Coast U.S. state of California has passed laws intended to reduce its total greenhouse gas emissions to 1990 levels by 2020. The province of British Columbia in western Canada has set a goal to cut emissions to below 1990 levels by 2020. The United Kingdom has proposed a 60-percent drop below 1990 levels for certain emissions by 2050.

Future agreements will need the cooperation of most or all countries to succeed. The Intergovernmental Panel on Climate Change (IPCC) is a committee of the United Nations. It provides scientific information to world governments about the impact of human activities on global warming and climate change. This information will help governments decide on future action.

Climate change affects
the entire planet.

GLOSSARY and RESOURCES

atmosphere The mass of gases that surrounds a planet.

atom The building blocks of the simplest kinds of matter on Earth, the chemical elements. Elements include hydrogen and oxygen. Each element is made of one basic kind of atom.

carbon dioxide A colorless gas with no smell, found in the atmospheres of many planets, including Earth. On Earth, green plants must get carbon dioxide from the atmosphere to live and grow. Animals breathe out the gas when their bodies convert food into energy. Carbon dioxide is also created by burning things that contain the carbon.

carbon footprint A measure of how much greenhouse gas a person, group, or activity adds to the atmosphere.

climate The weather of a place averaged over a length of time.

concrete A mixture of cement, sand, gravel, and water that hardens as it dries. Concrete is used for buildings, sidewalks, roads, dams, and bridges.

drought A long period of dry weather

environment The air, water, soil, plants, and animals on Earth.

exhaust The used steam or gases that escape from an engine or other machine

fertilize Adding any substance or chemical that makes soil or water richer for plant growth.

fossil fuel Coal, oil, or natural gas.

greenhouse gas Any gas that warms Earth's atmosphere by trapping heat.

habitat The kind of place in which a living thing usually makes its home.

heliostat A mirror turned to reflect the light of the sun in a fixed direction.

insulate To surround with a material that does not *conduct* (transmit) electricity, heat, or sound.

mass transit Public transportation, such as buses, trains, and streetcars, for large numbers of people.

mineral The most common solid material found on Earth. Earth's land and oceans all rest on a layer of rock made of minerals. Minerals also make up the rocks on Earth's surface.

organic Any of a certain group of compounds (mixture) that contain carbon atoms.

oxygen A chemical element (O) that is one of the most plentiful elements on Earth.

suburb A community next to or near a central city.

subway An electric railroad running beneath the streets in a city.

technology The tools, machines, materials, and means used to produce goods and services and satisfy human needs.

turbine A propeller-like device that powers a generator.

watt A unit of electric power.

Books:

Caduto, Michael J. *Catch the Wind, Harness the Sun.* North Adams, MA: Storey Pub., 2011.

Miller, Debra A. *Global Warming.* Detroit: Greenhaven, 2013.

Rothschild, David de. *Earth Matters.* New York: DK Pub., 2011.

Rusch, Elizabeth. *The Next Wave: The Quest to Harness the Power of the Oceans.* Boston: Houghton Mifflin Harcourt, 2014.

Tomecek, Steve. *Global Warming and Climate Change.* New York: Chelsea House, 2012.

Websites:

National Parks Service – How You Can Reduce Greenhouse Gas Emissions at Home
http://www.nps.gov/pore/learn/nature/climatechange_action_home.htm

United States Environmental Protection Agency – A Student's Guide to Global Climate Change
http://www.epa.gov/climatestudents/

United States Department of Energy – Renewable Energy
http://energy.gov/science-innovation/energy-sources/renewable-energy

United States Environmental Protection Agency – Climate Change and Waste
http://epa.gov/climatechange/climate-change-waste/

Think about it:

Geoengineering could help counteract the warming effect of greenhouse gases and make it easier for people to live with climate change. While some people support geoengineering, others fear it will produce too many major side effects. Some of these side effects could include: earthquakes, horrible weather, an increase in deserts, and floods.

Do you think the potential benefits of geoengineering are worth the possible risks? If yes, why? What could make such risks worth it for you? If no, why not?

INDEX